Slow Bruise

Aideen Henry

with images by Mary Avril Gillan

salmonpoetry

Published in 2015 by
Salmon Poetry
Cliffs of Moher, County Clare, Ireland
Website: www.salmonpoetry.com
Email: info@salmonpoetry.com

ISBN 978-1-910669-17-4

COVER IMAGE: *Untitled* from the 'Instances' series, oil on canvas 90x120cm, 2000.
By Mary Avril Gillan.
INTERIOR IMAGES:
"Passenger 2", oil on polyester film, 9x18 inches. By Mary Avril Gillan.
"Figure", oil on paper 9x19 inches. By Mary Avril Gillan.
"Passenger 1", oil on polyester film, 9x18 inches. By Mary Avril Gillan.
For further information please contact maryavrilgillan@gmail.com

COVER DESIGN & TYPESETTING: *Siobhán Hutson*
Printed in Ireland by Sprint Print

Salmon Poetry gratefully acknowledges the support of
The Arts Council / An Chomhairle Ealaoín

Acknowledgments

Acknowledgements are due to the editors of the following publications in which a number of these poems first appeared;

Southword, *The SHOp*, *The Sunday Tribune*, *Moloch Journal*, *Ourobouros Review*, *The Galway Review*, *Over the Edge — The First Ten Years* (Anthology, Salmon Poetry, 2014), *The English Chicago Review*, *Ambit*, *The Interpreter's House*, *Ropes 2014*.

The poem, 'Word Ancestors,' was a Prizewinner in the Seventh Annual Troubadour International Poetry Prize, 2013.

Big thanks to my fellow Galway writers for all their support and camaraderie.

I am grateful to the Heinrich Böll Association for the opportunity of protected time to write during the artist residency in Achill in July 2014.

Special thanks to Grace Wells for her sharp eye and encouraging heart and to Máirín Ní Dhonnchadha for her thorough attention to detail in the translated poems.

I am grateful to the Arts Council for granting me a Literature Bursary, which freed up time to work on this poetry collection.

Finally special thanks to the artist, Mary Avril Gillan, for use of the cover images and images used throughout this collection. They include life-drawing figures along with images from the 'Passing Throughness' and 'Instances' Series.

Contents

Trevelyan

Culvert

"You land, it seemed to him, on the shore of your own being in total innocence, like an explorer who was looking for something else and it takes decades to penetrate inland and map the mountain passes and trace the rivers to their sources. Even then, there are large blanks, where monsters roam."

JOHN UPDIKE, *Baby's First Step*

Spine

In memory of Siobhán Ní Shuilleabháin
1928 - 2013

I listen to a gaggle of women
persuade themselves
they're not ready —
the standard's too high,
their work isn't worthy,
it lacks depth, relevance,
their voice is too different,
it doesn't belong
in the bigger world…

I remember my mother
when a rejection came in,
tightening the twine
on yet more brown parcels,
sending out again
to other competitions,
other publishers,
kicking her heels up
that they thought they might stop her.
What do they know? she said.
What do they know indeed.

Endogenous

In memory of Jim Mhicín Ó Suilleabháin 1892-1973

What's it all for?
He asked each morning,
clambering out of bed,
rough-woven woolen trousers
over long-johns,
giving his porcelain legs
a thickness they didn't have.
A morning's work with cattle lifted him.
Lunchtime he hummed as he washed down
buttered soda bread with slugs of tea,
his nose disappearing inside
the blue and white striped mug.
By evening, egg yolk stained
the day's white bristle on his chin,
then to bed singing *The Rose of Tralee*.

Ón Áit Laistigh

In memoriam Jim Mhicín Ó Suilleabháin 1892-1973

Cad chuige in aon chor é?
A d'fhiafraigh sé gach maidin,
ag strácáil leis amach as a' leaba,
treabhsar olla garbh-fhite
anuas ar fho-bhríste fada,
cuma thiubh ar a chosa poircealláin
nach raibh iontu i ndáiríre.
D'ardódh obair na maidine leis na beithígh a chroí.
Am lóin, ag crónán dó fhéin
ag slogadh té 's arán donn 's im,
a shrón i bhfolach
ina mhug stríoctha bánghorm.
Faoin tráthnóna, guairí bána an lae
ar a smig smeartha le buíocán,
ansan, seo leis ina luí,
ag canadh *Rós Thrá Lí*.

Hiberno-English

So, what do you call the smallest pig
in the litter, in your parts?
It was his obsession
when she first met my father.
Rut, droigh, scrunt.

A bachelor until thirty-six and even after six children,
he always scalded the teapot for one,
boiled an egg for one.
At their first play together he left midway,
she nearly didn't follow.

How could you resist a woman
with that mountainous homeland in her nature,
he said to me later.
She never really left it,
forty-five years exiled in Galway.

She reserved its language for him,
for us her children and for dear animals.

Warming-Down

The rare treat of a
weekend with my father:
we sail to Inishbofin
on the Island Discovery.
The first inkling of the wind-down,
our stertorous walk.

Sínte isteach sa chlaí, traochta
ar nós Oileánach ag breathnú
ar ghliondar na dtonn.
He stretches onto the hedge, recovering breath
like an Islander witnessing
the visual feast of sea spray and rock.

Island home becomes nursing home.
Instead of books, the word-surgeon packs
a porridge saucepan, asks childlike questions,
rotates between meals and hearth,
and naps often, like a baby,
all scent of manhood gone.

Gone also the depth and breadth
of conversation, now on a short loop.
But his compassion and elation
escape vascular compromise.
He is happy to feel safe with me in this place.
Happy, sad.

Nomad

Is this the kitchen?
He says.
I thought he was joking
big man of my childhood
my gentle father.

I have difficulty with orientation
He says.
Astray in the house
he has lived in
for thirty-seven years.

Where will I put my things?
with laden arms
he asks
his wife
of fifty-two years.

He's okay
She says.
It's just his short-term memory
he's still himself.
I wish.

Living On

In memory of PL Henry 1918 - 2011

There is another man with his name,
living on the other side of town,
on another street of the same name,
in a house of the same number.
This other man lives the life
he has stopped leading.

His looped thoughts unlink
and open downwards,
they dibble deep,
tunnel under stone walls,
surface in the wrong fields,
or tail off in blind-ending passages.

His thoughts try to straddle the ribs
of long term memory,
to send tendrils that hang,
free ends curling, like fern, to corkscrew
and anchor remaining dendrites
before they can retreat from reach.

His consciousness basks there,
bathing in his repository
of childhood memory,
the adventures of the Tuatha Dé Danann,
of the many ways of saying a thing
and prelingual reverie.

Word Ancestors

What does he think, with no other language
behind his words, no translation,
no multiple meanings to decipher
all hints of intent, no cross links
to other drifts where his abstractions
can find a foothold in the deep cold flow,
wade to shore and hurl themselves
onto powdery sand banks
to desiccate and curl.

Instead words are flat.
Dead hyperlinks.

There is no footman with dry hands
to guide him to an open carriage
and trot him through the park
smelling of horse dung and silage
where he can lie back and regard
the vault of leaves and branches,
while glints of filtered moonlight
rush past him in the dark.

Focailshinsir

Cad a cheapann sé, n'fheadar,
is gan aon teanga eile faoina theanga fhéin,
é gan aistriuchán, gan cialla difriúla
chun gaoth an fhocail a aithint,
gan ceangal le ritheanna eile
a ligfeadh dá shaor-smaointe
greim coise a fháil
sa sruth domhain sioctha,
an cladach a bhaint amach,
's iad fhéin a chaitheamh
ar bhanc gainimh phúdartha
chun triomú agus caisniú.

Ina ionad san, focail leamha.
Hipearnascanna marbha.

Níl aon bhuitléir tanaí ann,
chun é a threorú isteach i gcóiste
agus bogshodar leis tríd an pháirc
mar a bhfuil boladh chac capaill agus sadhlais,
áit gur féidir leis síneadh siar 's breathnú
ar dhíon duilleog 's craobhacha,
fad a ritheann drithlí an tsolais scagtha ghealaí
thairis sa bhuandorchadas.

Nanometre

A Nanometre is the length a man's beard grows
in the time it takes to bring a razor to his face

The computer regards the space between words
as concrete, as if it were another word or letter,
though one that repeats often, singly
between words, twice after a full stop.

It counts the break between pages
as solid as if it were a line,
the break between sections
as significant as a title.

That which isn't
defines that which is.

Like seeing a person with all their dead relations
standing around them, nodding. The hairline from that uncle,
paunch from that cousin, aquiline nose from that aunt,
down-sloping eyes from that grandmother.

Though we can't see them,
they are in us just the same,
a bulge here,
a miss there.

Hors d'Oeuvre

You only get glimpses of the fullness of an emotion,
feel the presence of it pass behind the hedge
as you walk along, little practices for what's ahead;

seeing someone else's baby
lying still and wary
in the hospital cot,

someone else's son
stretched on a steel gurney
in the morgue,

someone else's father,
colour leached from his face,
not himself, in his coffin,

his waxen fingers
queerly intertwined
with rosary beads.

You shake these off at the time
and recognise them later when
the full surge of feeling breaks.

Black-veined White

And look, he said, what my mother has sent you for Christmas.
But she's never met me.
Exactly, he laughed as he gripped a white fluffy jumper
by the shoulders, a drunk hoisted for a mug shot.

A sparkling sequined butterfly across the chest.
Hah, he said, as he bunched it
and flung it in a ball
to the corner of the room.

Let's go, he said, and we pulled on our jeans
our woollen jumpers, our boots, and our raingear
and trudged to the pub for music and pints.

Later that night in the locked bathroom,
I pulled off my man-shirt
and slipped into the butterfly.

It shone light on my face and clutched my young breasts,
yielded to the points of my shoulders, wrapped its hands
around my waist, and shimmied over my hips
clinging to them beneath my jeans.

I folded it back in its wrapping and kept it.
I kept it until he was gone.
Until I was left with just me.
Then I wore it.

The Look

So rarely witnessed
I didn't trust my judgment.
Nope, couldn't be lust.
Too dark
for joy or love.

I am no good on absolutes —
give me a complex emotion
with its physical signals
and I will tease out
all the dominant parts.

But pure emotion confounds me.
I recognize only its beauty.

The look runs down her long nose
from her tilted-back head.
It starts at my eyes
and slowly works down my body
to my feet and back up.

Once it reaches my face
it flicks away.
It is beautiful.
It is pure.
And it is hatred.

I dodge the obvious
and bring a friend to diagnose.
'No question,' she says, 'she despises.'
'Me?'
'Not especially, no. But you'll do.'

Mouth Breathing

Pregnancy honed my sense of smell
so fetid breath reached me across a desk.
Perfume lodged on my nasal membrane
and bombarded me with its emetic fumes.
Mouth breathing, my only refuge
even when the source had left the room.

A plot of land on fallow ground,
is housed by an electric fence
skeletal horses amble around it
deterred by its multitonal hum.

A feeling grows behind a perspex screen
biologically mine but not of my moulding.
I cannot know it, protect it,
or spare myself from it.
Sometimes I sit next to it,
and light on its profile
with sidelong glances.

Pi

The 24 hour record I scrawled
in a sun-bleached ledger
during those first few weeks
of feeding my new baby;
the time she started,
how long each side,
the time she stopped.

Scan the wind
as it tugs at treetops,
or feel an irregular pulse
from a heart that has forsaken
its programmed rhythm;
when it no longer trusts
its intrinsic beat.

The rational mind tries to map
these sequences variable to infinity.
It looks for matches,
it looks for patterns,
it looks for sense.

Vulcan

Vulcan, sculpture by Eduardo Paolozzi,
Scottish National Gallery of Modern Art, Edinburgh.

I want to stomp through long grasses,
feel the brown bog squelch between my toes,
skate the lake's meniscus
then clink up marble steps
to the ting ting of metal tipped shoes.

Give me a soapbox on a street corner,
a burger hut where I'll fry onion rings
on wet nights in February
or a Fianna Fáil Cumann meeting
full of red faces, where plain words loiter and roam.

They showed me this box

Look, they said,
the lid so taut,
we can stack bigger boxes on top,

the sides so rigid,
other boxes will squash beside,
flush.

Big enough to contain
all they'll have me do for them,
and more.

Small enough
that I do not oscillate,
do not agitate,

do not reverberate,
do not threaten,
do not unbox.

Small enough
that I
do not really fit.

But no matter,
I can leave so much of me
outside.

The Practised Elbow

This is no mistake.

The smell of it first, flowery, pungent definitely bossy.
Then the feel of it, sharp and blunt if that's possible,
it carefully wedges into place between your ribs and hip
where your kidney sits without cover.

Once in position you feel the force behind it;
one sharp greeting
then the sustained poke,
as its body weight backs it up.

You follow the elbow to its source.
No, not towering above you but smaller.
The shoulder raised so the elbow's level with it
And the eye line just inches above that.

You turn your head
to locate it,
a cream-jacketed arm with large black buttons
or a navy woollen coat with silver embossed bobbles.

The owner, a woman with flicked back hair,
thick short fingers and tapering red nails
or a man with a wide low stance, a sweaty shaved head,
wearing a wide tie and a collar size too small.

The eyes look straight ahead.
You're only an obstructing kidney
easily dealt with.
If the dig weren't so insistent you'd pat that head.

You yield because that is what you do
and the elbow follows you into your give,
just to let you know
who's who.

For Sure

When I read her story
I know that could never happen me, I just know.

I'd never meet a man like that in a hotel,
have a few drinks with him, casual like.

I can't stomach cider anyway,
guts of steel she must have.

I'd never invite him back to my place
and no way would I sleep with him.

I don't have long hair
and who'd be caught with that colour in it?

And I hate the cut of them jeans.
and the rings? Don't talk to me.

And what's with the Chanel bag?
I mean, really.

And anyway,
my boobs are no way that big.

And I'm definitely taller than her,
skinnier too, like.

Lookit, our kids are the same age
and we're both on our own but

that's where the likeness ends.
For sure.

Caretaker

It's a queer place to live inside this skin.

I extend into each finger,
compressing air,
fleshing out a glove.

Breathe into each lung,
wipe fluid webs from the corners,
exhale an alien cello tone.

Blow snow spray onto each hip,
to lubricate and stretch,
buffer against the load.

Splint each vertebra,
chain link the spine
as it accordions onto itself.

Draw up each shin
forever sliding down,
like slack tights.

I resist the constant drift to leave.

Squeezing out the Cloth of Self

The surface has writhing parts,
elbows and hips protrude,
like a body trapped behind a curtain,

or a baby as he creases
his mother's abdomen
with a knee from within.

While a newborn fasts between feeds,
his eyes track his mother
about the room.

Once it reaches full pitch,
I am back there again,
responses as before.

Always the end at the beginning.

Lattice

A sheep's skull on my shelf,
sun-bleached,

scorched dry of soft matter
by the suck of the sea.

His horns point downwards and
backwards,

like bird wings at rest
or two guns sheathed.

Aligned holes in his face for
nutrient vessels,

sentried portals to a walled town
allow supplies in and out.

My face is riddled with
bullet holes,

reticulate, fenestrated,
patterned like lace.

Sinuses laid bare,
moist membranes sieve air,

traffic through unchecked,
more space than scaffold.

Spindrift

*"I believe Icarus was not failing as he fell, but just
coming to the end of his triumph."*

JACK GILBERT, *Failing and Flying, Refusing Heaven*

Beer flows into the glass,
the froth brims, then drops
lacing the inner glass.

A cake rises in the oven,
curls and crusts over the tin's edge,
the centre sags on cooling.

Forget depth.
Depth's gone.

Cut to kindness
and good cheer.

Lure

"Cloud formation, birds, driftwood and ice-glare in the sky were all clues to the whereabouts of land, even when it lay beyond the horizon."

DUBLINIA,
Viking & Medieval
Exhibition, Dublin

Premature Intimacy

You answer the advert;
you are lonely,
you are blue.

How tall did you say?

Yes, love can go into hiding,
and not visit for years.

Green eyes, that's nice.

So you gave up on meeting 'the one',
like you quit county football,
once you knew you wouldn't make it.

You seem warm, easygoing.

Your longest line, seven months:
truth, your defence;
you did not love her with all of your being,
so you left her.

How long is your hair?

You prefer telly to reading.
You've watched friends marry,
for children, companionship,
occasionally for love.

I have all of my teeth.

We know only first names.
You insist you're very genuine
as though there are grades.
Now the four walls close in on you.

It doesn't seem worthwhile
to set the table for one.

We speak on the phone,
in the quiet of the night
from two hollow houses
one hundred miles apart.

And so we will meet;
see what life has done to each,
of the stories we've threaded
see what proof lies in the flesh.

The Opposite of Denial

A puddle forms on a table
from the teapot with the dribbling spout.
I run a finger to open a path
for its controlled escape
like the flesh snip of an episiotomy
that sound of cutting silk
a deliberate release
so the tear is predictable
the spill steered.

ATNA (All talk, no action)

He crashed on my couch, an unrestrained front seat passenger, low impact collision.

Your tongue, he said. Give me more of your tongue.

Suspected whiplash, minimal restriction of movement, no tenderness.

Thank you. Now please, sit on my face.

Incongruous request. Disorientation? Confusion of body parts?

Oh, feck, no way. Tea maybe? I have mint.

I want to suck your toes.

Regression? Certainly poor discrimination and impaired judgement.

Here, my fingertips, will they do?

I want to come inside you.

Grade I concussion, maybe grade II.

I want to make love to you.

Ara, Jesus, why didn't you say? Come on so, what's keeping you?

Hot Sheets

I slacken my arms from around your chest,
slip my chin from your shoulder, stand still
trapping moist air between us and watch in the mirror
as you answer the phone to speak with your wife.

Yes, of course, very busy, a meeting this morning,
dinner last night, oh the usual you know,
hotel beds so uncomfortable, see you love,
yes, late evening I'd say, see you.

You turn to face me, no lie in your eyes
and on your way to the door you forget we are two,
your wife and I,
Goodbye love, you say, Goodbye.

As though I am wearing her dressing gown,
as though I am the part of her
that has forgotten
it yearns to make love with you.

Outside and In

The splendour of you
spread across my lap.
I tongue your velvet,
your vellum
like the moist soft gills
of a wild mushroom.

I am unfolded,
laid out for you
to probe and invade
my every place,
so that I wear you,
outside and in.

Ripe

I want to be brimful of baby,
overflow at breast,
pendulous and heavy.
with exuberant moist flesh
like the vivid innards
of a soft ripe plum.

I want to be hostage
to the echo of your pleasure
and harbour it until it can find
breath and wind to sail by.

Geallta

Irish for promised or engaged

I feel wedded to you
in a way no ring could encompass,
nor love child consolidate,
no break-up could sully,
nor dark words tarnish.

You are within me,
in a place your probing parts
will never touch,
a cool template to my magma,
an inner breastplate to my core.

Unrequited Pathological

I am jealous of the air he breathes and displaces,
the water that washes over him,
lingering randomly
in horizontal bodily fossae,
the mirror he peers into,
the comb that traces his hair pattern,
the aftershave that lingers on his face,
the clothes that variously enfold him,
the socks that envelope his awkward toes,
the leather shoes his feet give shape to.

I am jealous of the ground
that meets his outstretched foot,
the seat he yields his weight to,
the leather bag he grips purposefully,
the business he attends to,
the friends he embraces,
the colleagues who relate so casually.

I yearn for
fights unfought,
love unmade,
children unborn,
depths of mutual knowing unreached.

I wish to know him
with all of my senses.
My world is beige.
My feelings unchanged.
Time does not heal.

I am jealous of the air he breathes.

Crucible

I zoom out

away from your apple scent, your crumpled dry skin,
back from your elbows blanching on the glass table,

from your smile that buries those eyes, the flesh above hangs heavier
as you describe leaping from the scorching third floor of your marriage,

from your prickly lip-brush against my cheek
outside the car park, as my fingers stroke your waist,

back from the street your car drives down,
whatever car you drive.

I zoom out

so all the street colours wash out to grey,
all streets to pencil lines, arteries with white,

white blood sucking through them.
The town retreats then the country.

I perch on a satellite, outside your vector field,
relieved.

Extrication

What's mine and what's his?
How to sever without leaving part of me.

How to undo his intimate knowledge
now unbearable.

How to take me back, discard shared beliefs
and smooth over the rents of detachment.

Like when a placenta abrupts,
its footprint bleeds on the inner womb,

or when burnt skin peels away
to reveal new skin beneath, the same yet different.

Surprised by swells
of acute sadness.

Relieved to be back to myself.
Which self?

The conscious override
that navigates a safe course

or the elusive underworld
where disparate emotions

bubble up
from depths unchartered

like gases surfacing randomly
from thick simmering soup.

A Garland of Freshly Cut Tears...

Leonard Cohen, *Take This Waltz*

You sent me your socks.
The parcel so heavy
it might have been body parts.
What could it mean?

That you'll go sockless forever without me?
That life with socks is no longer worth living?
That you cried bitterly into them each day since I left?
That the world'd be a better place without socks and or me?

That we, the socks and I, deserve each other?
That you'd like me to wear them in your memory?
And your malevolence, shall I wear that too?
Maybe your shoes, toenail clippings or vests will follow.

I'm surprised you sent anything at all,
when you couldn't give me back how I loved you.

Impervious

I looked for you on the Dublin streets today
imagined

that while I walked along the cliff edge of pavements
you would drive by.

Or that your head would soar above the clouds of heads
and see me striding on.

That you would read over my shoulder
as I browsed for books.

I wanted you to see me strong, whole again
like when I trusted you.

I wanted you to see all your avenues to me
closed.

As though you
had never been.

Relent

Do they not know
that war is easier than love?

That with much practice
you can navigate every pretend hurt
and manoeuvre and screech your worth
until the outer layers
of their ear drums scorch.

That war is seductive as no love ever was
that you can come back and come back
and look for more ground, different ground
when their back has turned and that you can confound
so they don't know where they started
or what they want. And nor do you
but you never say.

That you know this place.
You've lain on its floor,
felt its cold tile against your ribs
watched its dust particles drift and settle.
Not able to leave
even when light beckons
through the open door.

Thunk

You carry around
the stinking carcass,
I no longer
recognise.

Dissect pathology,
in anatomical detail.
Spikes of blame
from stagnant pathos.

You beat me with
your strangled love.
As though
you had no hand in it.

As though I have no feeling,
or revival is still possible
after putrefaction.
Bury it.

Swahili

You speak, I answer
in the habit I learned
with someone else.

I understand what you say
from what it meant
from the lips of someone else.

I expect to hear nothing new
though you are new.
I want more of the same.

Why can't you be more like …
and rankle that you are not.
Though I am glad you are not.

My auto reply needs a reset.

Flyleaf

"Our hearts, bruised fruit from an aching stem"
CD Wright

My thoughts are in the silences
between words, the white space
between paragraphs, the flyleaf
of before and after.

These weeks and months,
an archive of events
we might have shared,
ridicule me.

Who did we think we were?

A Shorthand of Sensation

*"I feel an urgency to paint. Images come out the way they
are supposed to. I don't know what they mean. They are
a shorthand of sensation."*
    Francis Bacon

In the unconscious things people do
they give themselves away;

tossing loose tea
into a scalded teapot

from the pinch between
thumb and four fingers,

inhaling slowly
before turning a door knob,

tracing fingertips along
a freshly shorn neck,

repeating a story
with the same voice inflexion at the turn,

the same look of pleased surprise
at the end.

Just as my sagging abdomen
missed the baby

once curled, cramped
in its tight compress,

then unfurled, uncoated
of his vernix of me

in scratchy clothing
moved to his drawer

where his free limbs
clawed the air

in the continuous motion
of an upended beetle.

So too my inner eye misses
the purity of the loss of you,

as you lie before me now
your feelings streaming

down the walls,
your words crumpled

at the foot of the bed,
our pockets

outwardly filled
with each other.

Subsistence

When you turn the wheel to full lock
you only have to hold
for the car to keep turning
in the arc of that curve.

When you gain an extra four stone
you only have to eat normally
to retain
that bulk.

When you get used to reaching
over the shoulder of sadness
to set the dinner table
you can easily forget
it wasn't always there.

Scintilla

A line in iambic pentameter is said
to last one full breath.
Not yours.
I sit on your hospital bed
as you break mid-sentence for air.

I remember the smell of your scalp,
now shiny and bare.
Talk is of children, wills and schedules.
We never touch.
Too much passes between us, even so.

Rites

The travellers know it,
know how to feed it.

Big rosettes of flowers
in the shape of his name,

father, brother, cousin, son,
a gravestone where he died,

motorway, hedge, stone wall, canal.
Three days of a funeral

then every month
a death ritual for a year.

They know too there's no ignoring
this uninvited stranger in your home,

you feed, bathe and clothe
make him comfortable,

carry on regardless,
get used to him

because he's in the place
of the one that's gone

and he's not
leaving.

Searmanas Báis

Tuigeann an lucht siúil é,
tuigeann conas é a bheathú.

Fleascanna bláth
i gcruth a ainm,

athair, deartháir, col ceathrar, mac,
leac uaighe san áit ar cailleadh é,

mótarbhealach, fál, balla cloiche, canáil.
Sochraid ar feadh trí lá

ansan gach mí
searmanas báis ar feadh bliana.

Tá 's acu chomh maith nach féidir neamhaird a dhéanamh
den strainséir gan cuireadh a fhanfaidh leat as san amach,

tusa á bheathú, á ní,
á ghléasadh, á dhéanamh sócúl,

go leanann tú ort beag beann air,
go dtéann tú ina thaithí

mar gur thóg sé áit
an duine atá caillte

agus níl sé
chun imeacht.

Month's Mind

There's a piece
of me
in that coffin.

I cannot dismount,
unharness,
unlove.

I cannot unthink what I know
he will think of each thing
I see.

What he will say in reply
to each thought
I speak.

The part of my mind where his thoughts
and responses live,
remains.

Its neural mirror, my being within his,
now untwinned,
liquefies.

I am now the sole receptacle
of what was
us.

Cuimhniú Míos

Tá píosa
díomsa
sa chónra san.

Ní féidir liom tuirlingt
ná an grá
a scaoileadh.

Ní fhéadaim gan smaoineamh
ar a smaoineodh seisean
faoin uile ní dá dtugaim faoi ndeara.

Cad déarfaidh sé mar fhreagra
ar an uile mhachnamh
a labhairimse.

Maireann an áit i m'aigne
ina gcónaíonn a smaointe
is a nathanna cainte.

Anois, gan a leathchúpla,
leachtaíonn a scáthán néarógach,
mo áit in a aigne.

Is mise an chomhra aonair
don domhan fairsing torthúil
a bhí eadrainn.

Kindling

Feeling has no switch.

A woman drives slowly
in the dark past the house
of a man she once loved.

A man two decades later
remembers she never liked
lying her head on his shoulder, after.

A woman opens old love letters,
surprised by their immediacy
their urgency, their live currency.

You cannot unlove.

Trevelyan

"In dreams, images take the shape of the effects we believe they cause."

COLERIDGE

Dali in London

'Venus intersected by drawers'
empty drawers from head and heart gape open,
nothing hidden, free from care.

An elephant's reflection
thick-skinned solemn solidity
contrasts with the frivolity
of the paddling swan.

Christ on an invisible cross;
all the pain people carry
when the ordeal is long over.

Moonless

In memory of Monica Narciandi Junco, 1972-2011

A blind woman listens to the choir
she fingers her bracelet like rosary beads,

pressing the gemstones between thumb and ring finger
then rolling them to middle and index

like rubbing butter into flour
to make coarse crumbs.

What do her fingertips divine
from the indentations and crevices?

Do they sense that black
has less heat to give, white more?

Her eyes blink and wash clean the surfaces
light passes through,

light that never finds its way
to her seeing brain,

never reaches her moonless consciousness
where chant and fingertip sensations frolic.

John Montague, a drawing

The trapdoor of his mouth
lengthens to a smile

that lifts both cheeks
into upturned half-moons.

This closes his rheumy eyes,
rolling his view

in on himself,
bringing mirth.

He peeps out at us
for some sense

like an explorer from a tent
checking a blizzard.

His eyebrows rise and part
like flappers in pinball.

His bog-cotton hair, as amorphous
as wool before it is spun.

His nose, a boned tongue
long and sculpted.

His ears, tubular
with a hint of pixie.

Two spade-like hands
steady him on the podium.

Dun wool and corduroy
sheathe torso and limbs.

He moves about
in quiet tan shoes

and tells us how his past
blows through him.

Rats

Rats run behind the skirting of my home
During the day they disregard my keyboard clicks;
only when I speak or sing do they shush
and when we sleep they shorten their incisors, gnawing wood.

I trapped a rat today;
He opted for Wensleydale with cranberry over French gruyere.
My son found him, checking the cupboard twicely.
The children craned acringe from the stairs.

I shouted 'Hello, mouse, are you dead?'
and nudged the trap with a sweeping brush.
His free arm swung a slow arc through the air,
his digits spread gently on the floor.

He lay quiet, all his concentration
on his shoulder crushed in the trap.
His chest pulsed breaths,
eyes closed, white bristled chin up.

All thoughts of Orwell to the fore,
I moved him to a bucket with a croupier's slide.
I groaned as he landed.
Do rats groan?

His mate lies dead beneath the floor,
unable to clot
exsanguinated
not smelling yet.

Tulca

Irish for wave, gust, gush, outpouring, flood, deluge.

Sacrum and sternum in gold,
both keystones, crowns of arches,
reciprocal.

They embrace pressure from each side,
disseminate impetus, uncoil movement,
crossways

up through the body from the kicking foot
or down from the throwing arm
symmetrically

through the body when the butterfly kick
pitches head and winged arms
up out of water like a rising angel.

Goliath

Goliath lumbers down the hallway
my filing cabinet hoisted on one shoulder.
Weekdays, he works in a paintshop
mixing colours, looking over the heads
of worried housewives as they go on and on.
Sundays, he helps his Da,
a retired builder from Ennistymon,
with neart Gaeilge
and a van costing him nothing.

They transfer the innards of rooms across town.
'He's half-way recovered from last night'
smiles the Da, as Goliath palms
sweat through his sticky hair
before taking another box aloft
like a waiter a tray.
In the finish he watches his Da
pocket the notes, the fee not half
of what Goliath drank last night.

Amulet

Sad news undoes
the recently-spun shawl.
How frail the construct.

Cored hollow,
useless, internal
skirmishes between

ill-defined adversaries,
are like bickering children
plucking fistfuls of hair.

Better to find an outer amulet,
shave my head or
run around howling.

Surface tension

gives a drop its beaded shape,
a spill of water its curved edge,
a fountain its shimmering sheets,

causes liquid to collect itself to itself,
consolidate to take up the least space,
pull its skirts together from the gases around it.

Freed by detergent
bubbles disperse in the air
rainbow tides on their surfaces.

Undertow in the Everyday

Raindrops on the windscreen coalesce.

Tree roots nudge up tarmac,
crack open pavements.

An old lady teeters in heels
to the corner shop.

Virginia creeper worms between bricks
so the wall careens toward the street.

In a café, a fat man shovels in more food
not hungry but it'll do.

Longings manifest.

Menace Attracts

The raw meat of it,
the crush-clinch of muscle

as it bears down,
the purity of its chaste fury.

If you could reach in and touch
its quivering fillet,

uncouple it from its intent,
harness it, turn each clout

to a spanner-knuckled neck hold,
its fingertips would cradle your crown,

its slender thumbs fan your windpipe.
Torsos sweat-slicked, two lathered fighters

in the embrace pause of a final round.
Encircle it with your arms, legs and spine,

absorb its flailing elbows and hoofs,
ride out its bucks,

yield with it into each toss,
until finally it tires.

Fists unclench,
fingers interlock,

it lets you be
with it.

Scrios

Irish for destroy, erase or ruin

Laced
trussed

garters
bustiers

fethered
tethered

crotchless
thongs

frilled legs
forearms numbered

ankles shackled
masks on.

Human meat
wank with it

stamp the turkey
gut it

string it up
dress it

play with it
until you don't recognise

the living breathing
don't know what

you are eating
fucking.

Percept

A child with impaired hearing comprehends the world
from the sounds that reach her
no awareness of those that don't.

You don't believe you could be subsumed
until you look into that tiny face
and know it.

You don't know unsympathy
until sitting on the floor of your life
you feel the imprint of that boot
on your hand.

You have to keep the glass clean,
the glass through which you look,
so you see the world as it is,
not as it might be.

Mutability

Sometimes my fingers reach to my forehead,
in search of my son's scar,
into my armpit for my daughter's skin tag.

Sometimes I cough their father's incomplete cough,
my tongue falters behind my incisors
to whistle my first-born's lisp.

Sometimes I write my father's emphatic copperplate
or hover above the line in my mother's rapid light cursive
unable to resist their swirls and curlicues.

Sometimes your inept jokes sprout from my tongue
my friend's harsh look comes over my face
or my lower lip rolls in as desire curls yours.

I don't know myself with all these people.

Habit

I hitched a lift
on the russet Isle of Mull,
a kindly man stopped.

We exchanged truths
safe that we wouldn't meet again.
His wife had died seven years before,

he'd spent five years grieving,
then moved to Mull,
remarried, was happy since.

'Did you learn a lot in those five years?'
'Nothing at all' he said
'except the dull routine of sadness.'

Space

It starts with schoolbags on the stairs.
'I'm not having this' she says,
out they go, pegged out the landing window.
Lunchboxes disgorge sticky apple butts,
black bananas skins and silver wrappers.
Schoolbooks splay, words spill across the paving.
The pencilled scrawl of sums and handwriting
flitters in the breeze, notes home about cake sales
and holidays, speared by brambles, then sucked
under the privet into that windless place
where small birds dart.

Next it's the space around her.
Children, animals, her husband
all rushed out the front door,
no ifs or buts.
The cooker, the fridge, the built-in kitchen.
uprooted to the garden in their original formation.
Soon the rooms are clean of furniture.
She commandeers the kitchen-living room,
whips down the blinds, seals the chimney
squirts foam in the gaps between door and architrave
screeches masking tape around the drafty windows.

'Now', she says 'I'll have a bit of peace.'
And with a look of supreme serene
she inhales all the trapped air in the room,
her body tumesces and every cream pie,
pastry, éclair and doughnut she ever had
mobilises from exile and every chocolate torte,
pavlova, coffee sponge and banoffee she lusted after
joins them, cramming and straining the flesh of her stomach
stretchmarking and mushrooming her succulent limbs
until her skin slicks against the sweating walls,
leaving tiny air pockets in the corners.

Blanket Stitching

Unlit Santa Claus and reindeer lights on shop fronts
wait all year round for Christmas.
Like the reawakening of quiescent desire
or the latent chime of a toy
choked back by its wrapping.
From memory my friend rewrote a story,
then found the original, a twin,
its trail smocked on the lazy beds of his hippocampus.

Buying Santy

My son's eyes widen when he sees the trolley
full of toys the young couple push down the aisle.

'Are they buying all those toys for their kids and
pretending it was Santy?'
I nod.

His first Santy-free Christmas.

Difficult for him to believe,
though he knows this is truth.

Like the hard looks I gave each man I passed
in the months after my marriage ended.

Cicatrix

The glass eye doesn't double-take when I pass his seat,
then return its attention to his newspaper,
doesn't crinkle when he smiles into his phone
or when he slaps his thigh, laughing.

The glass eye doesn't peer into his coffee as he drinks,
doesn't wink at the waitress to flag her down,
doesn't swing side to side as he pats his pockets,
doesn't squint to pick loose change for the tip.

The glass eye stands proud and cool
sucked into its socket by tepid moist flesh.
Though part of him, it remains apart from him,
unreachable, insentient, imperturbable.

Laudemus

A gleeful boy kisses puddles
then mauls his friends
outraged by their laughter.

The relentless surge of wind-assisted
high-tide as it slams against
a wall of rock.

The calm urgency of a sprinter in slow motion,
her face drags as it lags
behind undulating footfall.

The relief on a patient's face
the unsaid is finally voiced
not curable but manageable.

Collect your love and kiss the ground.

Pocket lint

Dust particles and threads
adhere over time,
lint settles and collects.

So at any one moment
we see it as a cluster of something,
an entity.

We assume intent as if formed by design,
whereas unplanned and transient,
it has settled for a bit.

Like a person and their apparent depth,
a semblance of self,
fashioned from an engirdling mould.

It's a stray collection
cast together,
in this shape, at this time.

NOTES

Endogenous
Depression was formerly described as either endogenous or reactive. In endogenous depression, low mood was perceived to have come from within, without any external traumatic life event triggering it. In reactive depression, low mood was precipitated by a stressful life event, such as loss or bereavement, the change in mood a reaction to the major stress.

Living On
Memories are not stored in our brains like books on library shelves, but must be actively reconstructed from elements scattered throughout various areas of the brain where they were laid down. Long term memories are stored as groups of nerve cells (neurones) that are primed to fire together in the same pattern that created the original experience. In dementia, nerve cells become damaged or die and so do not transmit the required electrical signal necessary to retain and retrieve memories in the normal way. Dendrites are the branching extensions of each nerve cell, they enable it to link with other nerve cells to enhance transmission of electrical signalling which enables thought to take place.

Pi
The human heart has an internal pacemaker which sets the rhythm of the heartbeat and so sets the pulse for life. This rhythm is normally regular, it speeds up for exercise and slows down during relaxation according to the changing needs of the body for oxygen. In certain heart conditions, a person's pulse is persistently irregular instead of regular. In this case the heart takes its rhythm from some other part of the heart less effective at setting the pace than its internal pacemaker.

ABOUT THE AUTHOR

AIDEEN HENRY lives in Galway and works as a writer and a physician. She was shortlisted for the 2009 Hennessy X.O. Literary Awards for poetry. Her first collection of poetry, *Hands Moving at the Speed of Falling Snow*, was published in 2010 by Salmon Poetry. She also writes short fiction and her debut collection of short stories, *Hugging Thistles*, was published by Arlen House in 2013.

ABOUT THE ARTIST

MARY AVRIL GILLAN is an artist and educator and lives and works in Dublin. She has exhibited nationally and internationally and has received awards for her work both as an artist and educator. She is currently a lecturer in the National College of Art and Design and her work is held in both public and private collections in Ireland.